What's New in Science

by Bud Grace

*aka R. S. Grace PhD

What's New in Science

By Bud Grace aka Robert S. Grace Ph.D.

ISBN 978-1727275261

Published by Squid Inc.

©2018 by Bud Grace58.

Forward and Dedication

Although the cartoons in this collection were drawn over thirty years before this publication, and although what's new in science may not be so new any longer, the scientists haven't changed that much. I should know, I used to be one of them. You can find me in the literature under the cognomen R. S. Grace. At least that's what my major professor and later boss, James Skofronick (aka J. G. Skofronick in the literature), called me in the Physics Department of Florida State University in the 1970's. Under his guidance we did some seminal work in low energy atomic and molecular scattering. As a matter of fact, twenty years after we demonstrated the existence of the Ramsauer-Towsend effect for helium on helium collisions, another group which neglected to research the literature, claimed to be the first to do so.

Several of the drawings of laboratory apparatus in the pages which follow bear a peculiar resemblance to the ones we used to build back then. Two of my old professors appear in one drawing. A good friend of mine who happened to be a brilliant organic chemist and I appear together in another. As a matter of fact, it was Dr. Rabenold who, one night, read my Tarot cards and predicted my future. He was spot-on. It wasn't long after that I abandoned physics and began drawing cartoons.

But Professor Skofronick taught me more than merely how to work in a laboratory, how to assemble and perform experiments, and how to analyze data. He once told me that the study of physics can prepare a person for anything. It requires dedication, diligence, hard work and creativity. He was right. He was not only a first rate scientist and mentor. He was, and still is, a marvelous human being. This book is dedicated to him.

WHAT'S NEW IN SCIENCE

The search for the magnetic monopole is narrowed to a six block area in southeast Bayonne

"Does anyone recall what I'm trying to prove?"

"No wonder it leaks. That thing's a colander."

"We got a few left over, folks – Who wants 'em?"

"That's Professor Heisenberg. He can never make up his mind."

"When are you going to tell us about the birds and the bees and the hydrozoan polyps?"

"Me? Mad? Yes! Yes! I'm mad! But I have tenure!"

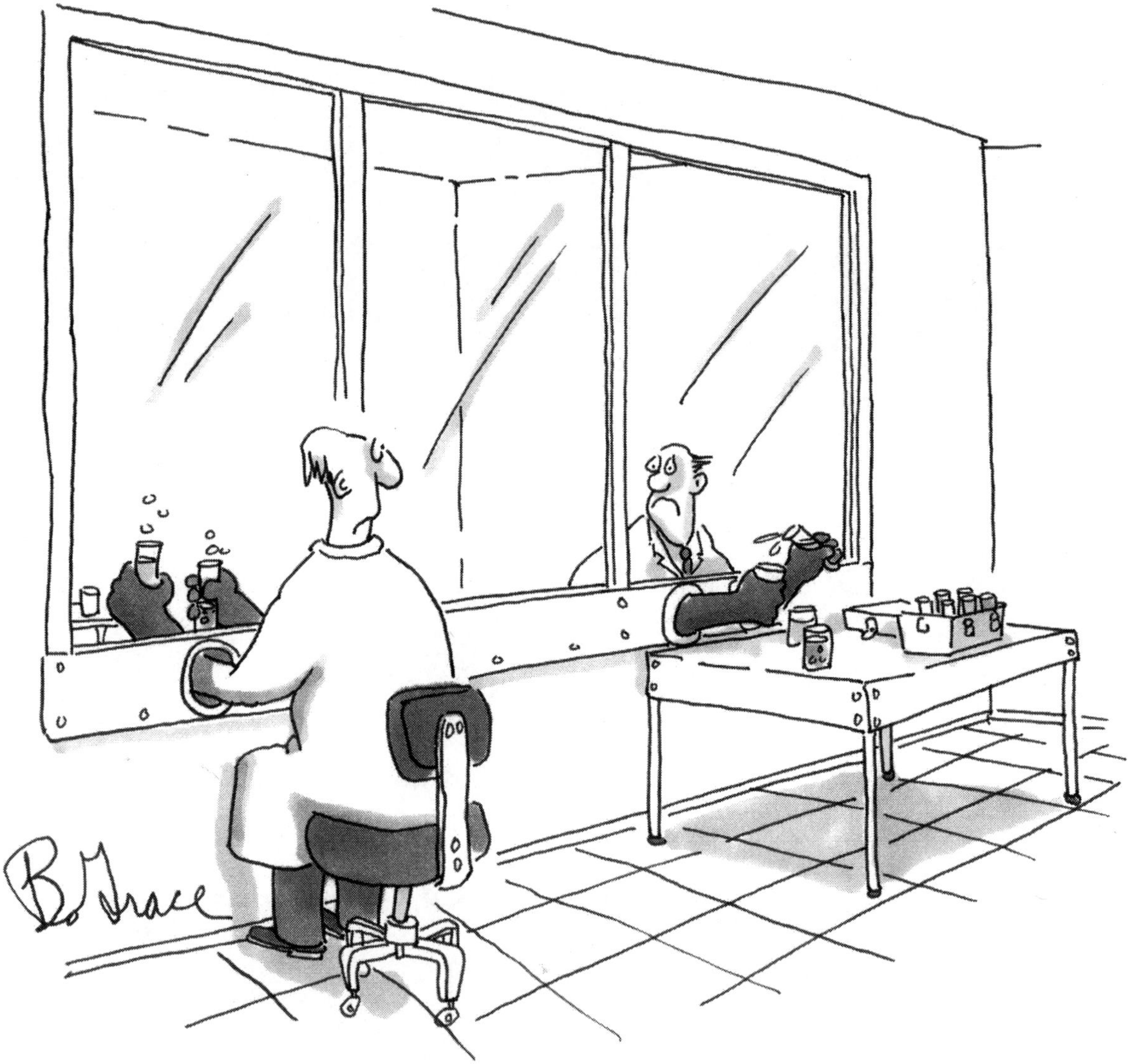

"**Now** will you admit that gravity is quantized?"

"Instead of the usual question and answer period, here's my version of a great Rogers and Hart tune I'm sure you'll remember."

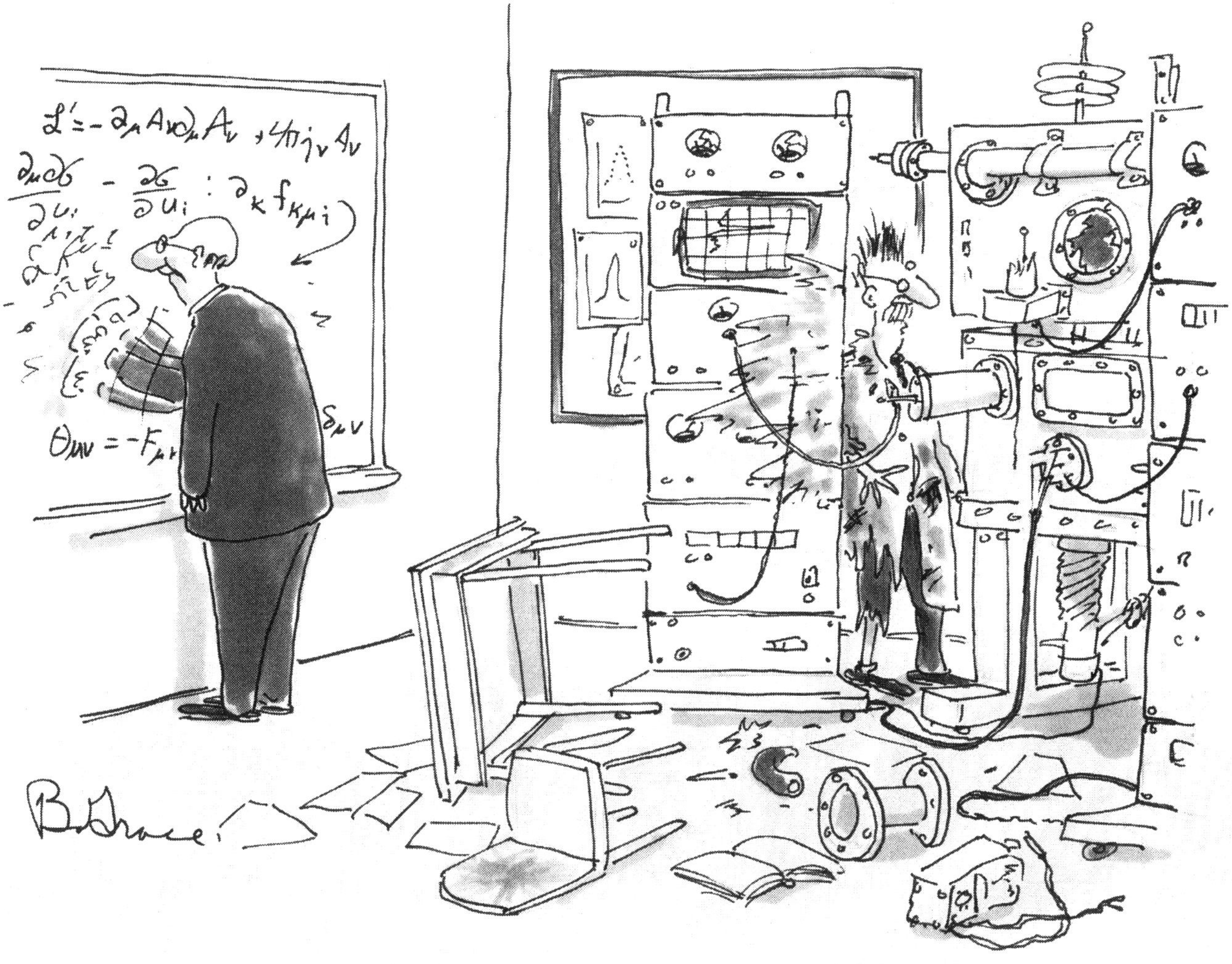

PROFESSOR EINSTEIN CELEBRATES HIS DISCOVERY OF THE THEORY OF RELATIVITY

"Now here's where the function of the hoplonemertean's rhynchodeum really gets exciting!"

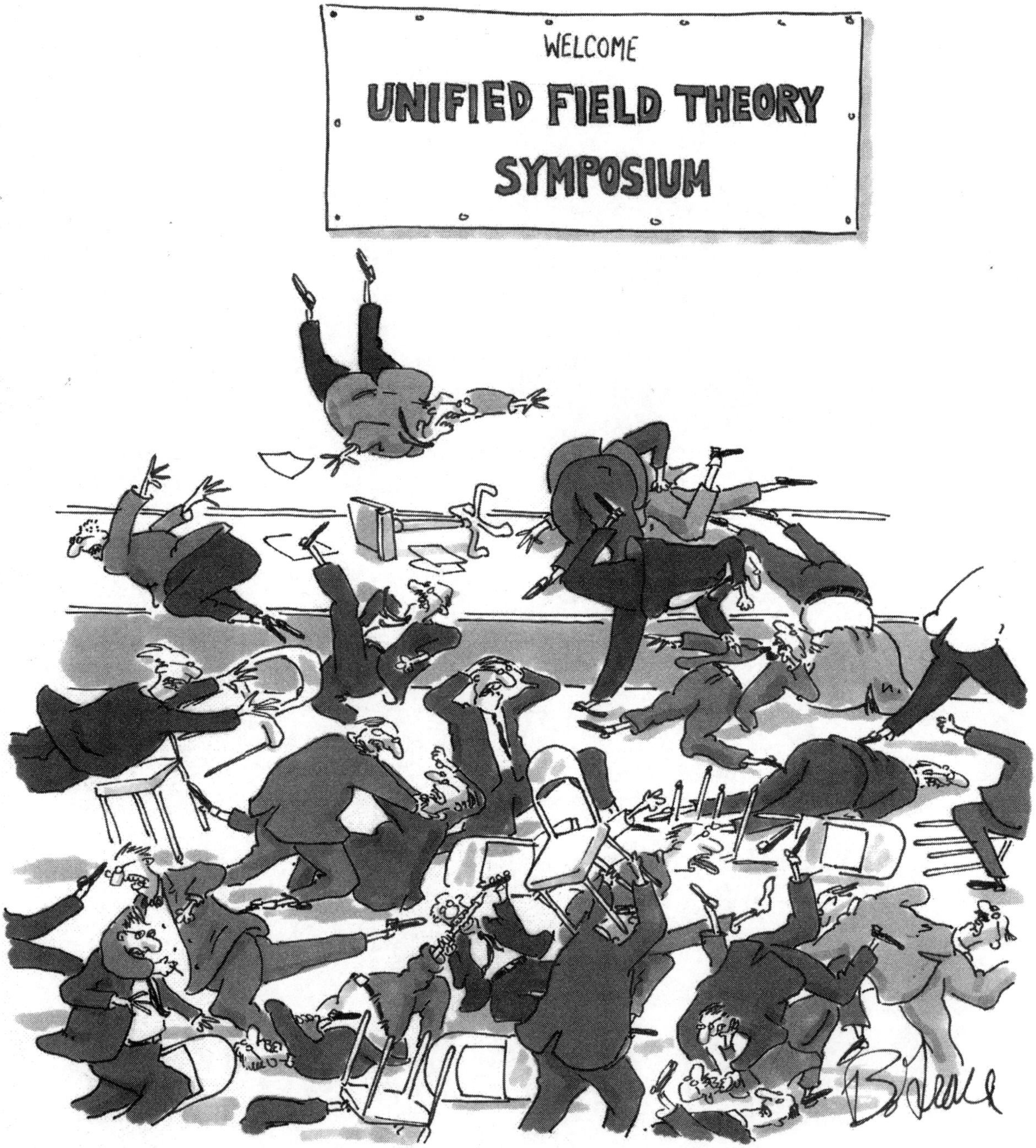
WELCOME
UNIFIED FIELD THEORY
SYMPOSIUM

"And what appears to be a pretty girl is actually a high energy laser holograph."

"Fred, we have to talk. I've been seeing another theorist."

"I regret to announce that this morning at eighteen minutes past ten o'clock, on the Cross Bronx Expressway, Professor Cramer was struck and seriously injured by a three thousand pound tuna fish."

"Don't mind me. I'm always self-conscious when people talk about sex."

"No more ticketing physicists, ok?"

"Linear? Who said it was linear?"

The Debate Continues

The Big Bang

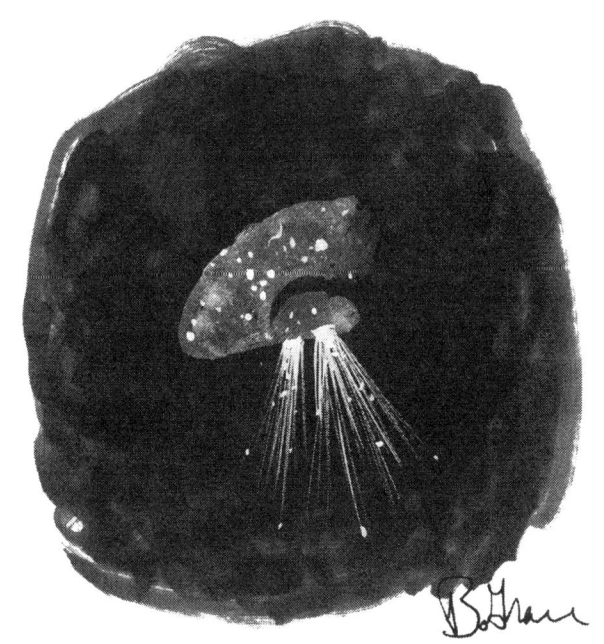

The Big Nose

Therefore
2=0

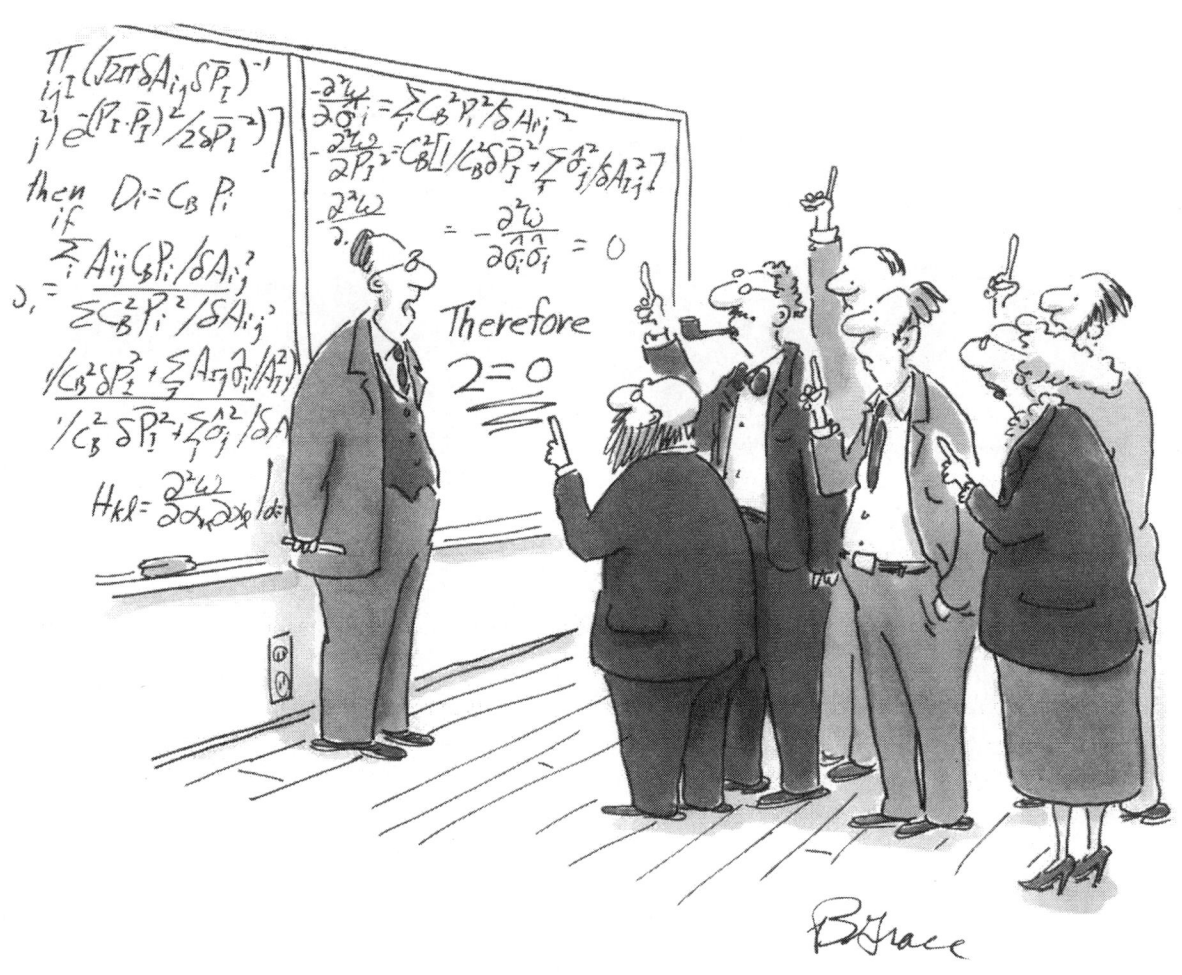

"Any Questions?"

"Alright, Henslow! Release Commander Ortega!"

"What we first thought was an antiproton sigma plus annhilation turned out to be linguini and clam sauce."

PAULI'S EXCLUSION PRINCIPLE

"They keep blowing up my microscope."

"God, how I hate grant renewal time."

"Eureka! Our antimatter generator is operational!"

"And the best thing we've come up with is an amoeba that oozes liver bile."

"Not only does this new baby check out, in the process it discovered a new prime number."

"Professor Huggins, of course, is no longer with us."

"Dearborn Street? Sorry, pal, this is the Batavia Accelerator."

"Steinmetz was testing his new infrared binoculars, and Miss Henslow came barging in without knocking"

"I was doing five to ten at Joliet. I knew I had to turn my life around, so I got a degree in physics."

"And do you, Professor Mulligan, promise to love, honor and co-author at least *four* papers a year?"

"It must be getting serious. They've been talking about fruit flies for three hours."

"Good news, Dr. Fishman - We got the rat grant."

Might As Well Dept.

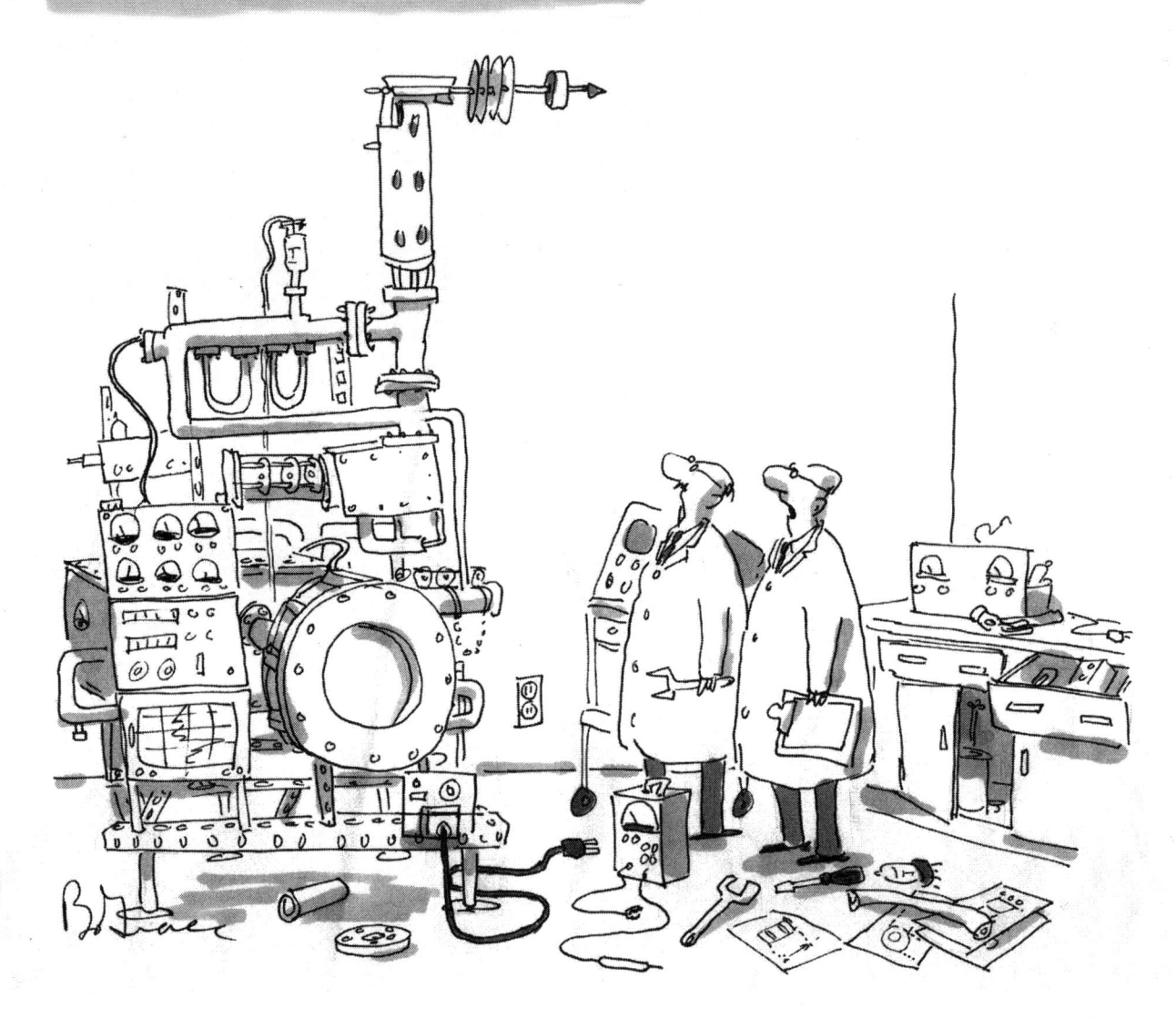

"Well, Stubbs, shall we drop it down the well and see if it splashes?"

"It's a new life form, alright. We found it growing in Steinmetz's coffee cup."

"Tragic story. He used to be a brilliant chemist."

"It's amazing, Professor Steinmetz, what can be accomplished with a $2 million government grant and a hundred pounds of Play-doh."

"Professor Morton is always careful to check his horoscope before taking data."

"OK, I admit you're very intelligent. But, honest, what I really like about you is your body."

"So much for laser communications."

"An impressive resume, Dr. Fishook, but just where is the 'Monroe Institute of Typing, Shorthand and Interstellar Magnetism'?"

"He invented television, digital computers, and microchips, didn't get any credit, and it's not going to happen again."

"Stop the movie! Stop the movie! Explosions don't go boom in a vacuum!"

MICROBIOLOGY PRACTICAL JOKE

"Nobody's going to believe it. I say we call it 'New Improved Ribonon with Deoxystat-Plus'."

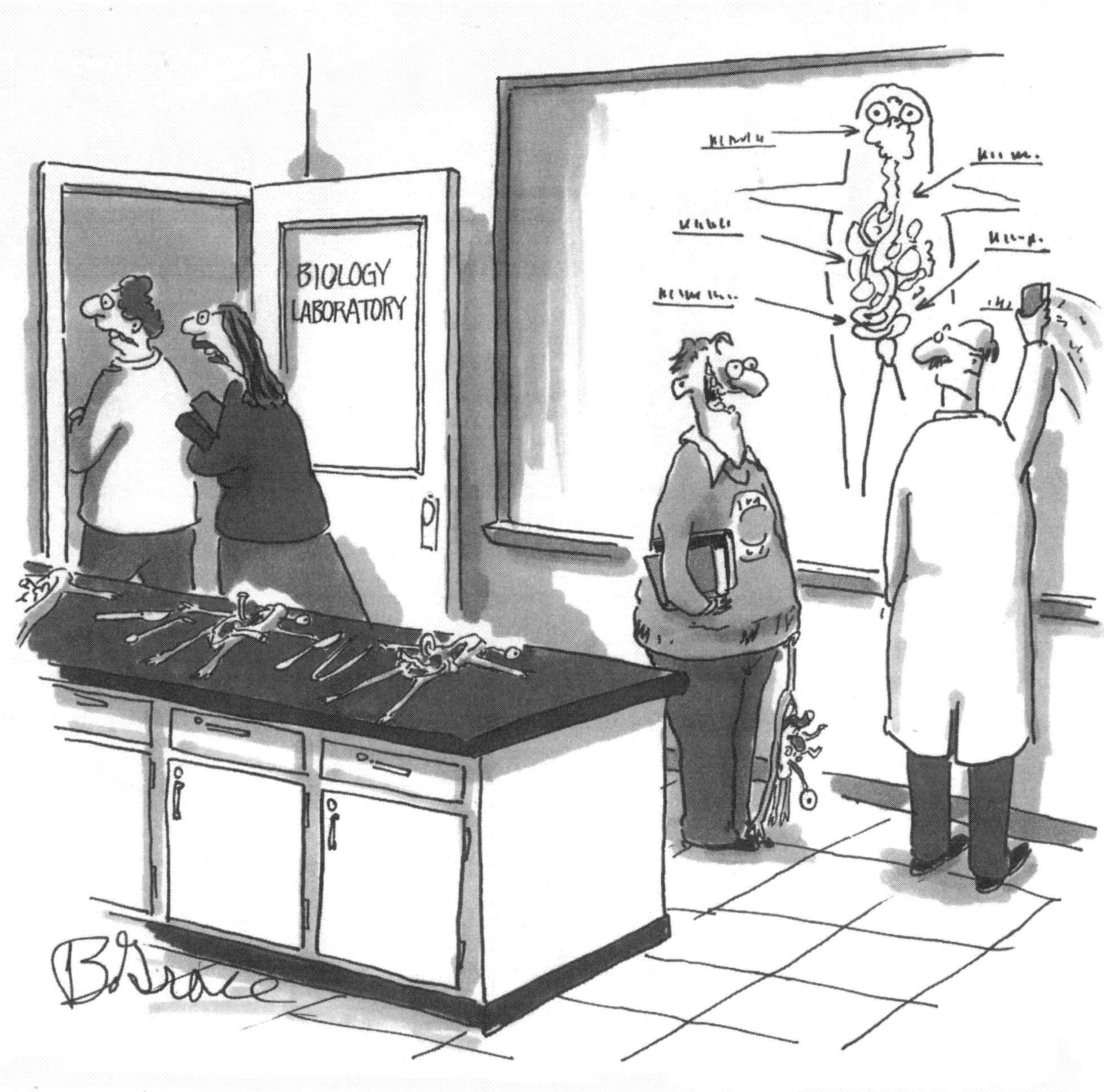
BIOLOGY
LABORATORY

"Can I keep my frog?"

Benjamin Franklin Discovers Electricity

"Ok, ok, I admit it. It's a toaster."

"Actually, we're here looking for husbands. If that doesn't work, we're going into nuclear physics."

"It's the same all over. Bernbacher thinks his wife is seeing another man but can't prove it. Professor Fernman thinks gravity is quantized and neither can he."

PROFESSOR WINSLOW DISCOVERS DR. CLAPPMAN FALSIFYING HER DATA

"Professor Hellbender likes to inject an element of humor into his experiments."

"It'll never work, Steinmetz. Where would we go for happy hour?"

"For pity's sake, Irene, can't you see I'm doing research?"

"Now I'm going to ask you all to close your eyes and pretend very, very hard."

GREAT MOMENTS IN SCIENCE

1898: Madam and Pierre Curie extract .0005 micrograms of Radium from 18000 Tons of Pitchblend

"See, high energy physics is a lot like bowling, only instead of pins flying out, sometimes you get a liverwurst sandwich."

"There goes our celebration."

"Wait a minute - I think I hear something."

"And the 10,000 kev peak appears because Professor Fishbane snuck up behind me while I was bent over the spectrometer."

"Professor Nussbaum, our abnormal psychologist."

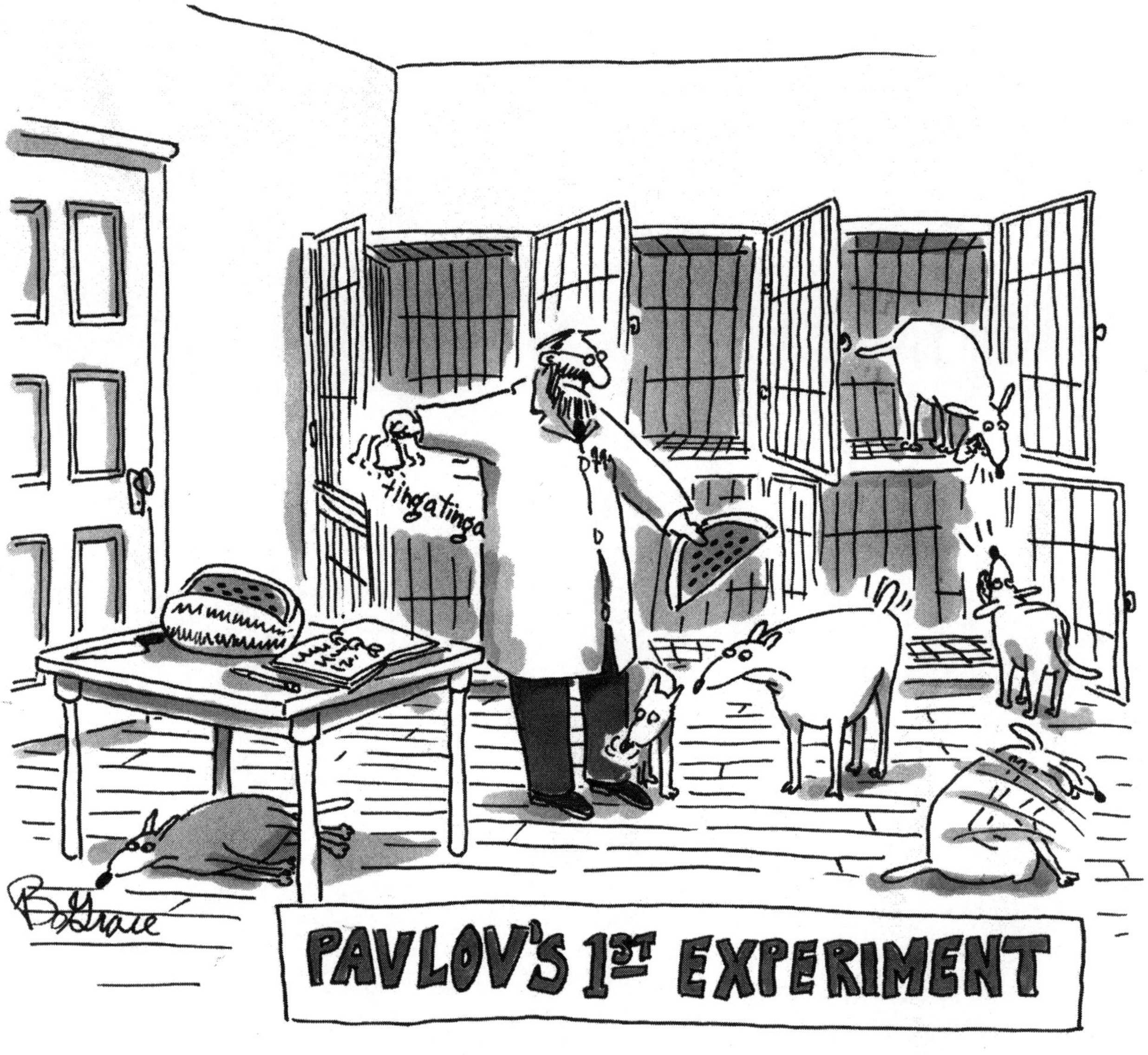
tingatinga
PAVLOV'S 1ST EXPERIMENT

fig1. White collar mice.

fig2. Blue collar mice.

"Who would have guessed that Ronco made a combination noodle spreader-electric quadrupole particle detector."

Let's see—black, segmented abdomen, 3 thoracic sternites, 2 jointed chelate chelicerae and raptorial pedipalpi— I don't know...
I don't know either, but one is crawling up your neck!

"Late again. As usual she'll blame the Heisenberg uncertainty principal."

"Interesting, but is it science?"

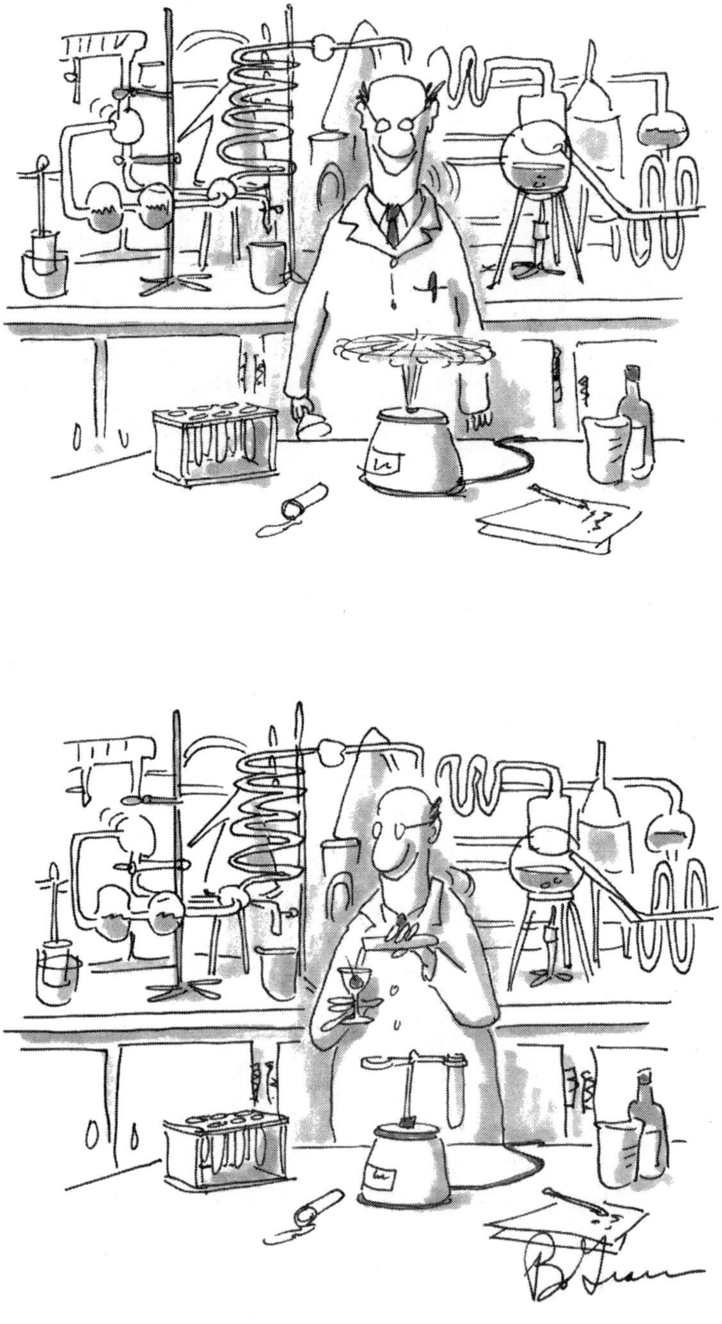

I believe there are COLORS that HUMAN BEINGS have never seen.
THAT, Ms. Boznik, is a PIGMENT of your IMAGINATION.
WHITE LIGHT
RED
ORANGE
YELLOW
GREEN
BLUE
INDIGO
VIOLET

"Miss Rosenblatt is my assistant, Gentlemen, not my experiment."

"We ran into a little trouble with our experiment, Dear. Don't hold dinner. Just leave some garbage in the sink."

"Sure I worked on accelerators before. I'm good on brakes, too."

"If this I.Q. test proves valid, his nose alone puts him in the genius range."

"What shall we work on this week? The diabetes cure? The Alzheimer's vaccine? The endocrinology reasearch? Or shall we take up where we left off last week and play Curly, Larry and Moe?"

"You realize if the university ever finds out we could lose our funding."

"One thing about working here - we have terrific coffee breaks."

"Sure he's not worried. He's already met his deductible."

"Then, according to Einstein, everything is relative?"

"Absolutely."

"Give the boy some help, Irene. Try to look stupid."

"First I want to thank our speaker selection committee for a job well done."

"We've about given up on computer simuation, scale modeling led nowhere, and the journals are no help at all. Pretty soon somebody's going to have to sit down and think."

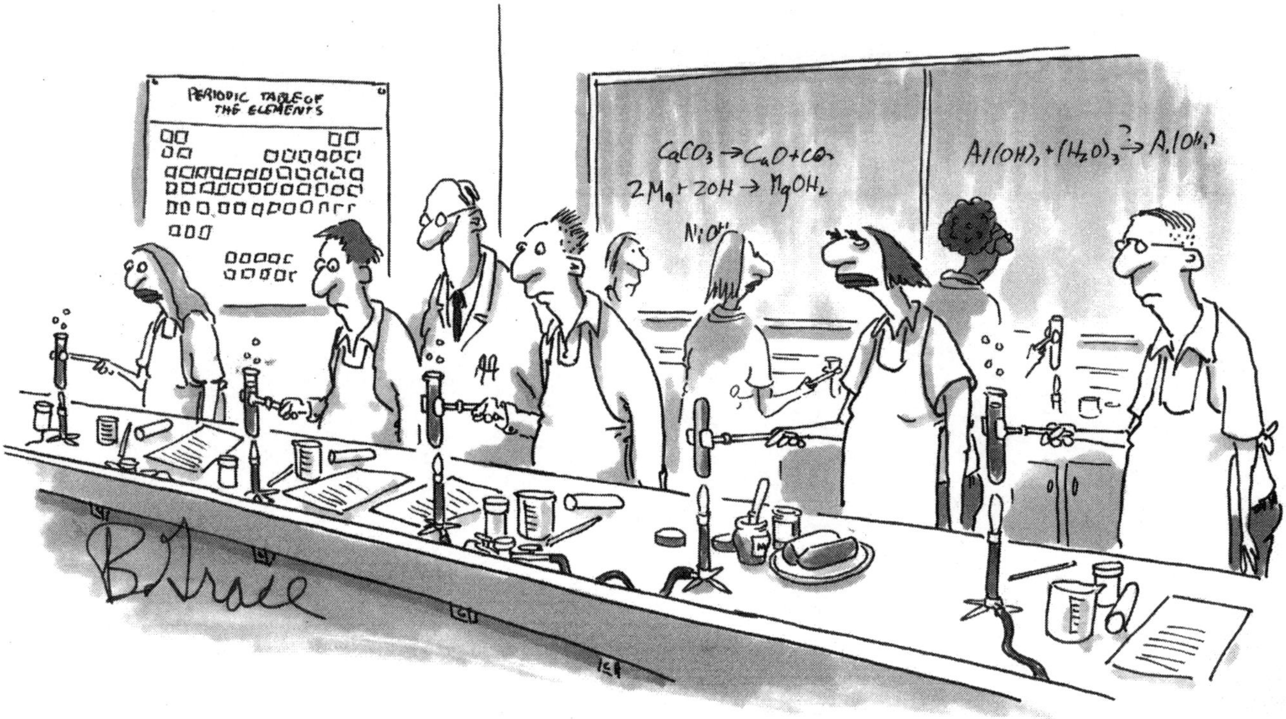
PERIODIC TABLE OF THE ELEMENTS
CaCO3 → CaO+CO2
2Mg + 2OH → MgOH2

"Congratulations, Professor Rabenold, you're finally beginning to make sense."

6 MILLION BC
4 MILLION BC
3 MILLION BC
2 MILLION BC
1 MILLION BC
504,000 BC
100,000 BC

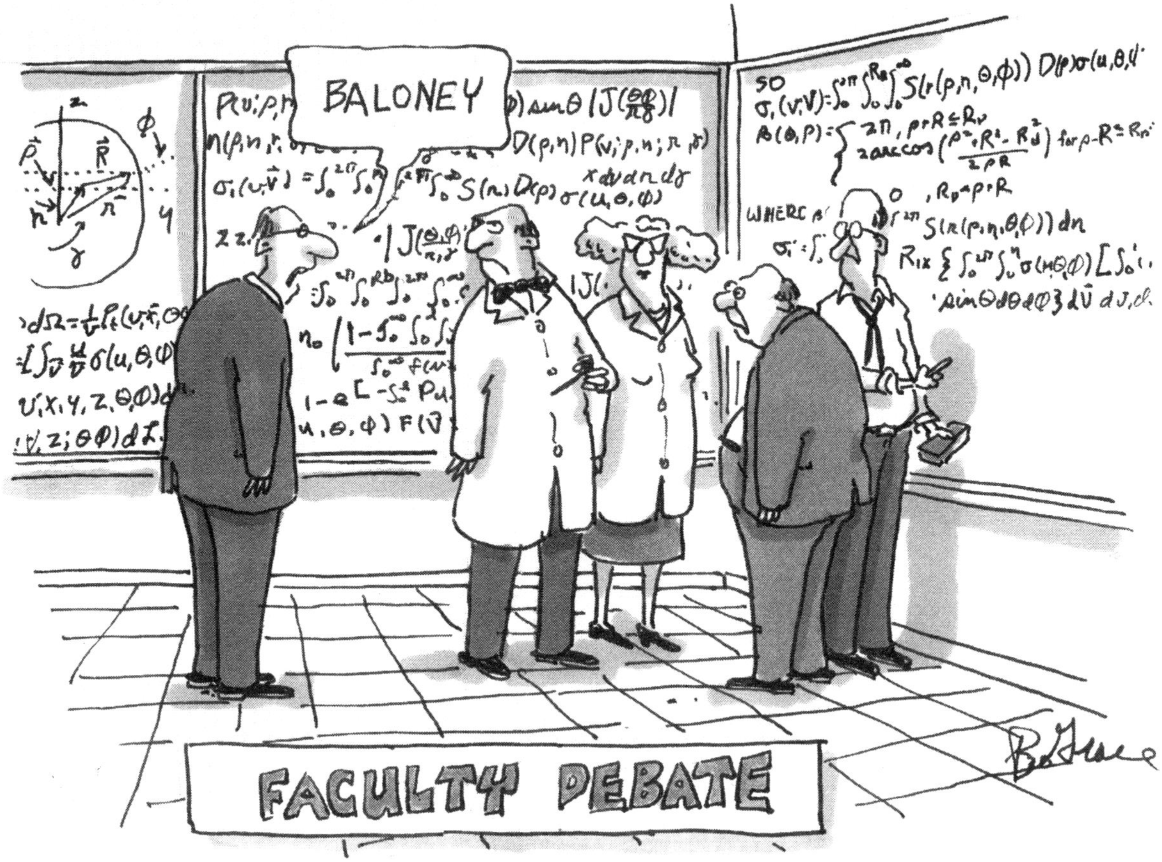
BALONEY
FACULTY DEBATE

"I disagree. My research shows that Cro Magnon was, in fact, intellectually inferior to Neanderthal."

GALEOCHERDO TIGERINUS!
Why Scientists Make Lousy Lifeguards
B.Grace

MORE TROUBLE OVER AT GENETIC ENGINEERING
And another thing...
The food stinks

SIR ISAAC NEWTON APPLIES HIS NEWLY DISCOVERED LAW OF GRAVITATIONAL ATTRACTION

"If she's such a genius, how come she named her new element 'Mickey Mouseium?"

MRS. FLAHERTY BEGINS HER ILL-FATED RETURN TO ACADEMIA

"Frankly, Hodgekiss, we were expecting a somewhat more sophisticated security access."

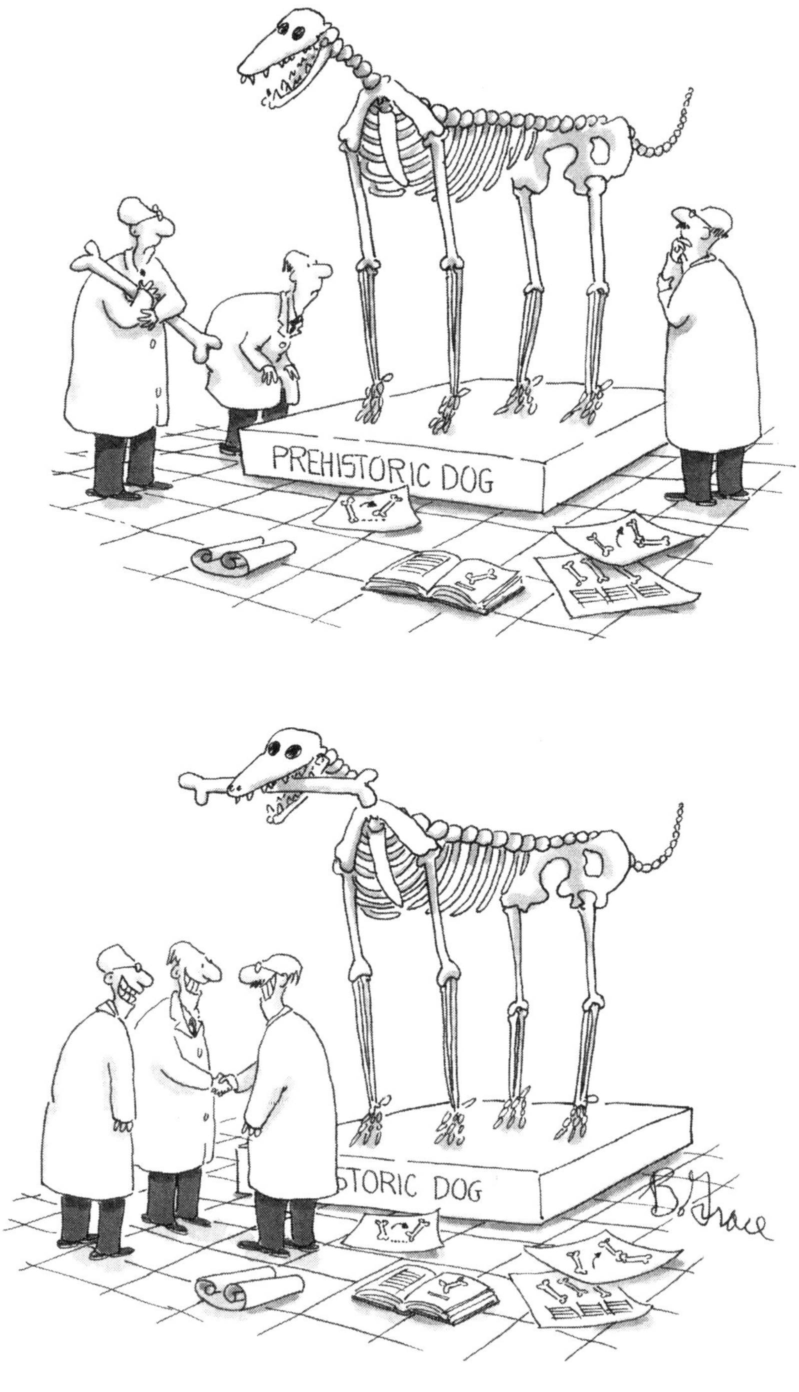
PREHISTORIC DOG
STORIC DOG

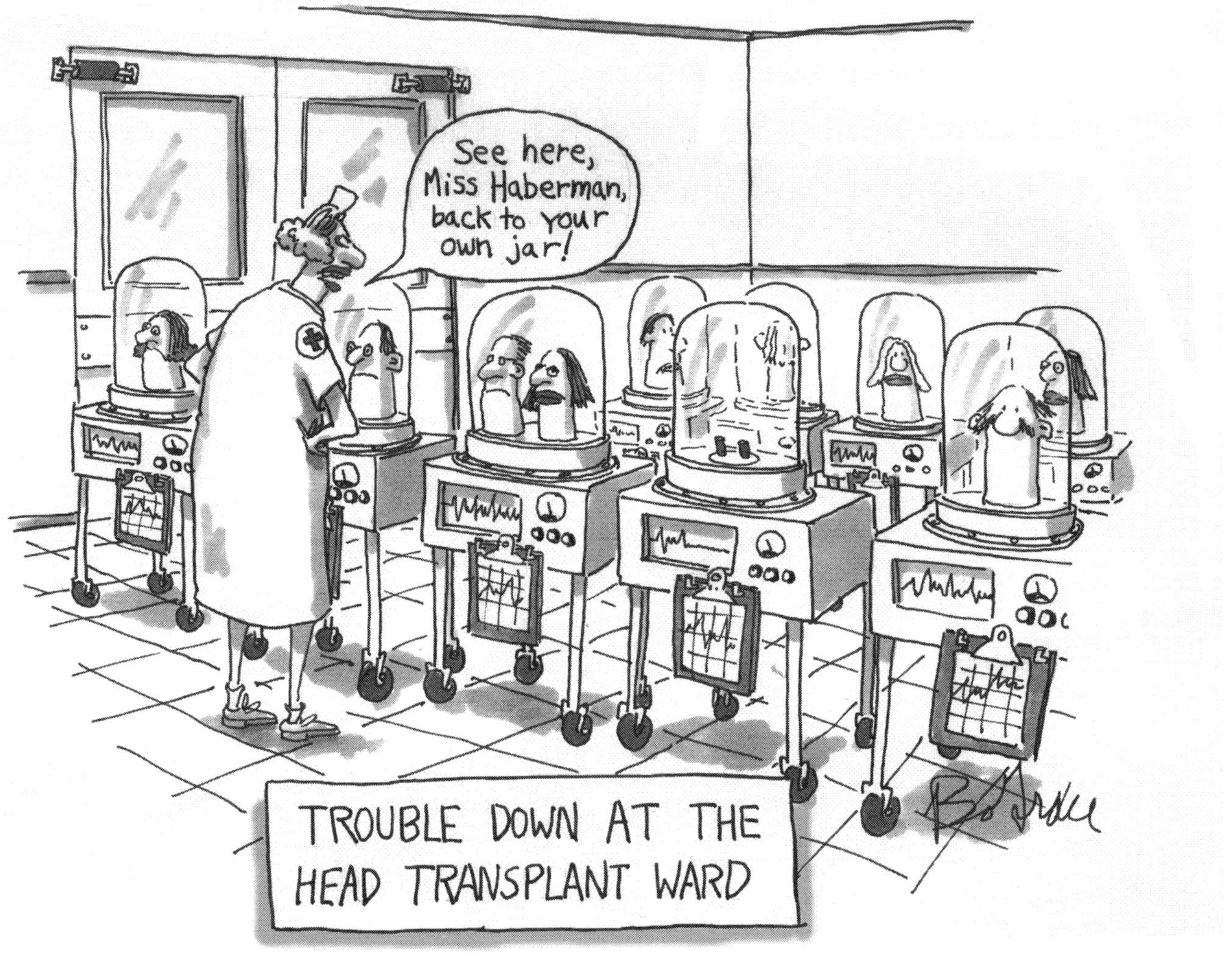
See here, Miss Haberman, back to your own jar!
TROUBLE DOWN AT THE HEAD TRANSPLANT WARD

Oh, Bernard, Bernard, can't you see it could never work? You're lepidoptera and I'm arachnida."

"No, Mr. Dorfman, carbon dating is not rolling around in a pile of soot with your girlfriend."

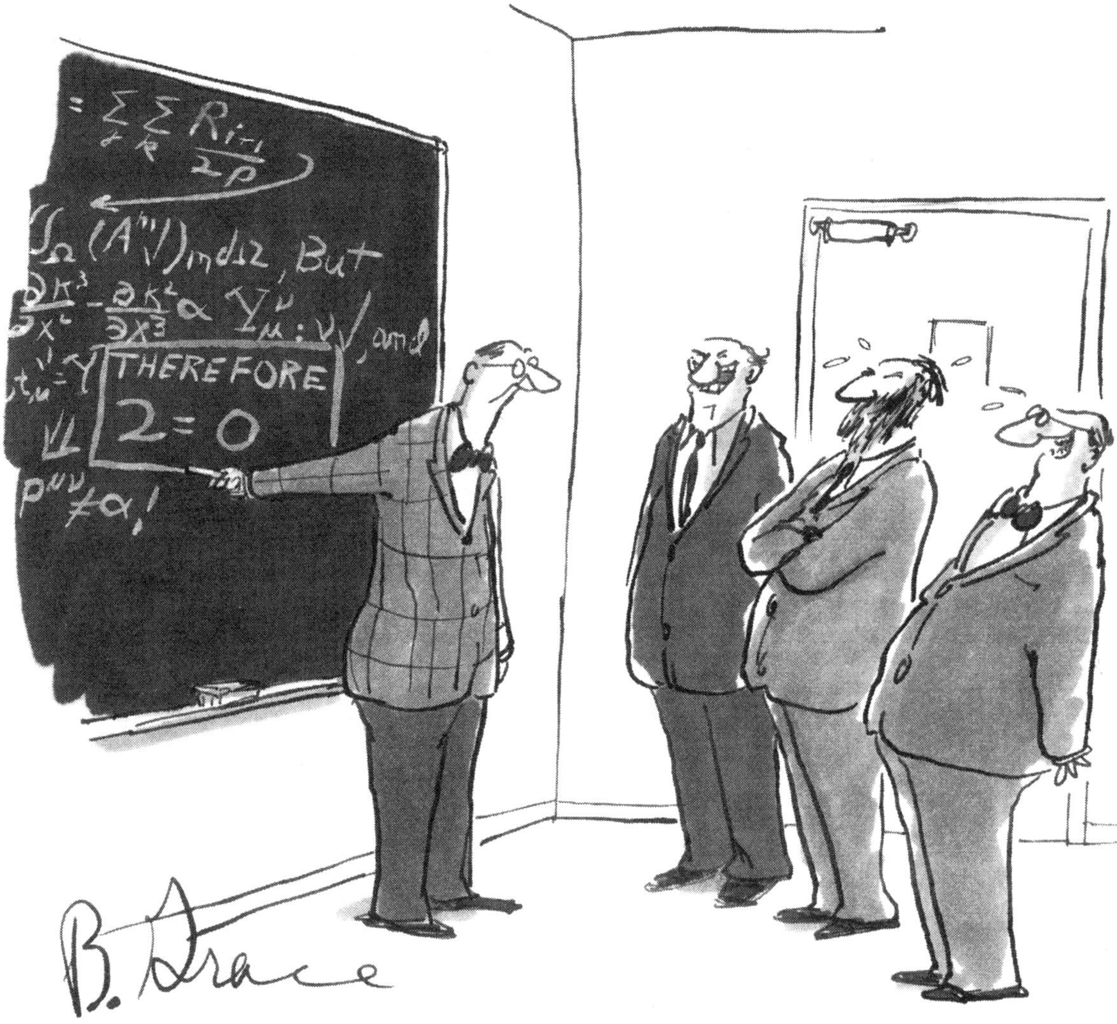
But
THEREFORE
2 = 0

"No problem, Professor, it's a holograph."

"May I remind you, gentlemen, that we're here to study anatomy."

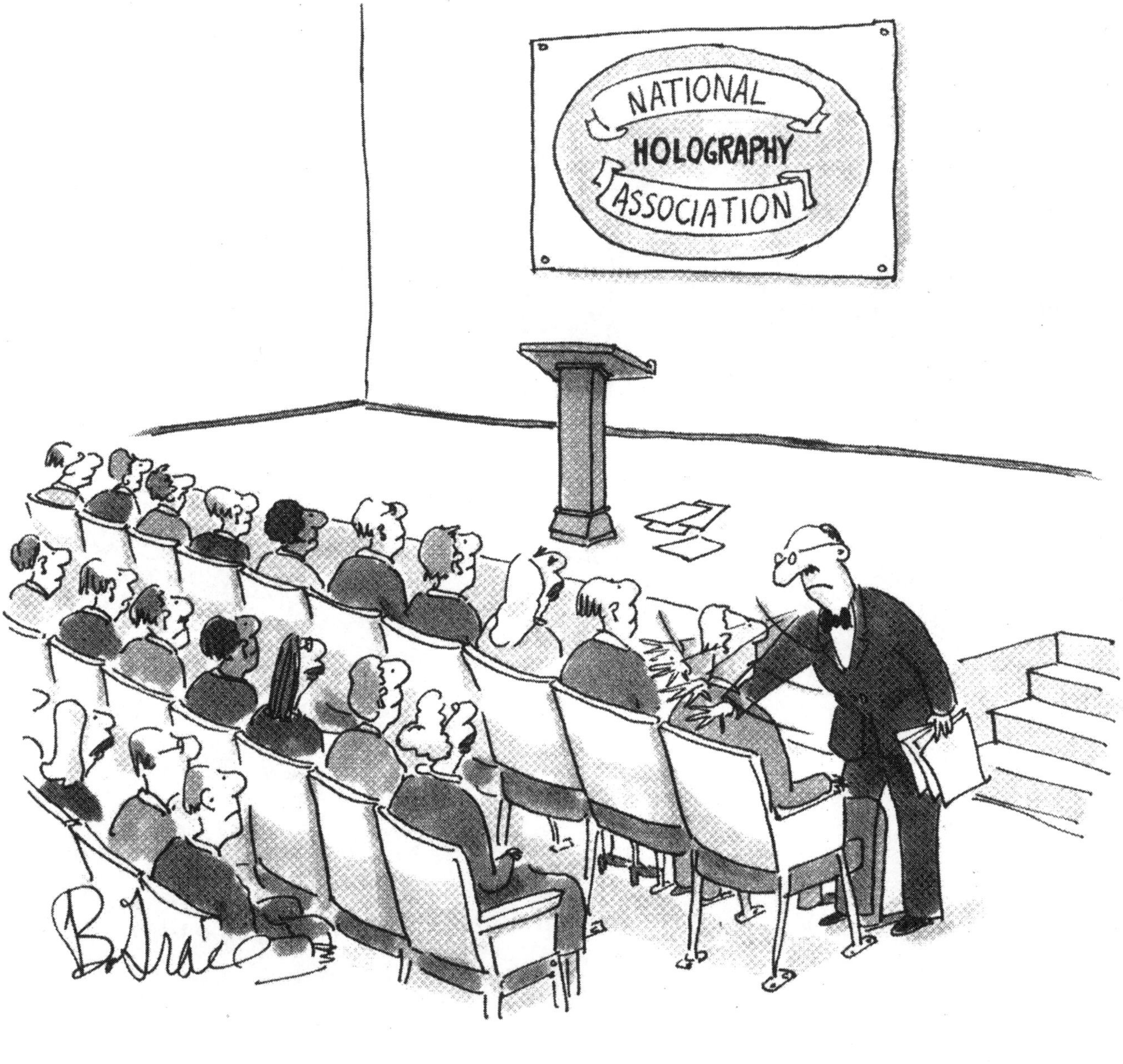
NATIONAL
HOLOGRAPHY
ASSOCIATION

MRS. E.I. DUPONT DE HENSLOW DISCOVERS SYNTHETIC RUBBER

"No kidding, I heard him say we weren't going to be used for experimets!"

"It's the one with seven electrons."

"Ergo, Professor Steinmetz, the overwhelming preponderance of mouse data."

Meanwhile, over at the Clone Research Laboratory...
DAMMIT, HENSLOW, ONE OF YOU IS FIRED

"Now do you believe in God?"

"But you're short, pimply and your glasses look like milk bottles. You must know something about differential calculus."

Philosophers

"But if God **DOES** exist it follows that the CARTESIAN IMMUTABILITY of the TIME-SPACE continuum coupled with the notion of co-lateral blah bla..."

"I'll drink to that"

"It is, therefore, my honor to award the 1983 Nobel Prize for Genetic Engineering to Loni Anderson's father."

"Belonged to a little old lady. Only used it once a week to balance her checkbook and remind her to buy cat food."

"I think I discovered a flaw in your logic."

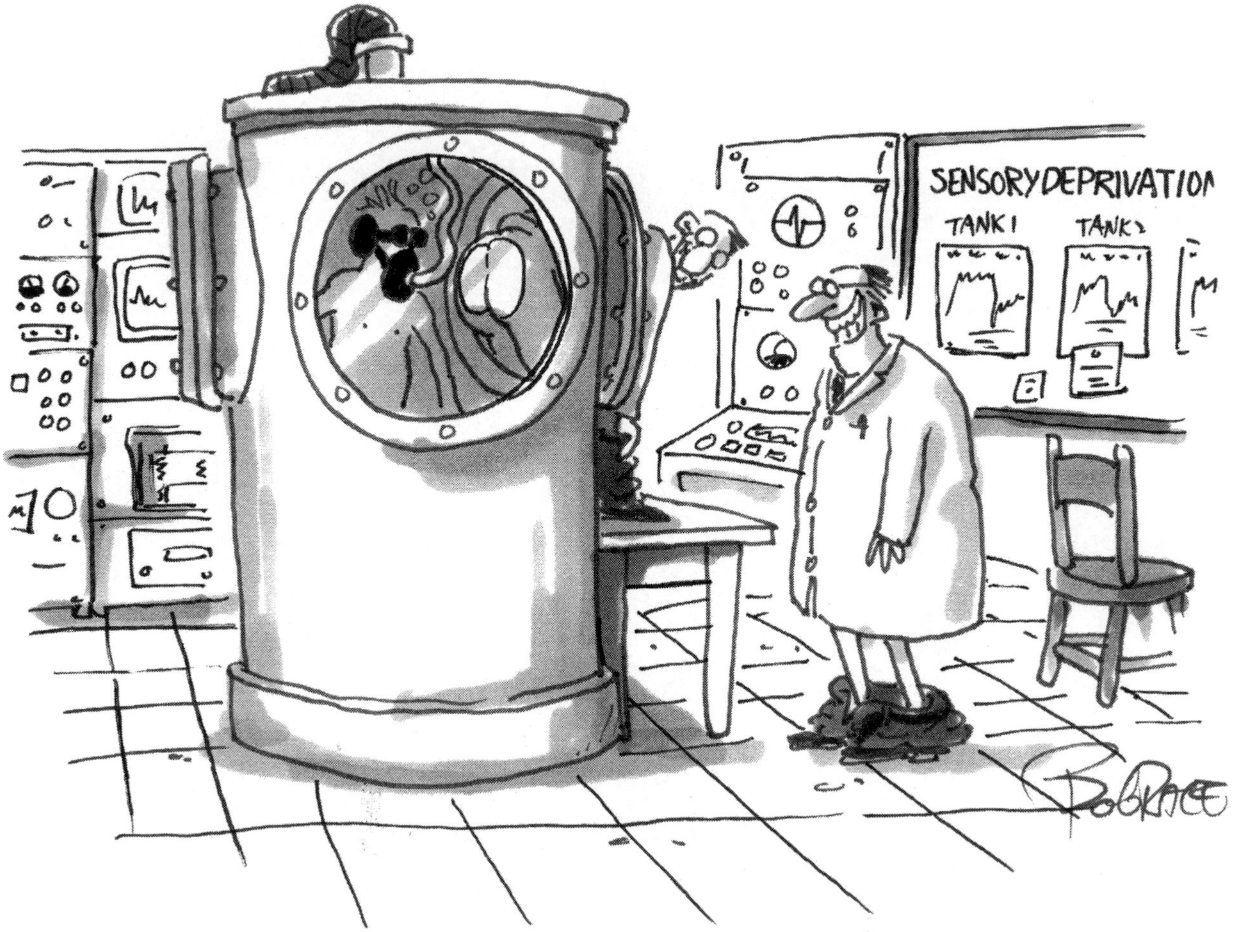
SENSORY DEPRIVATION
TANK 1
TANK 2

"Wait a minute. That isn't the Crab Nebula. That's Ed and Doris Wyman."

"Professor Steinmetz refuses to use his extraordinary intellect to design instruments of war. Fortunately I was able to convince him that this thing's an infrared surface-to-air cheese spreader."

"Professor Bernbacher works in catastrophe theory. Professor Henbaulm is our experimentalist."

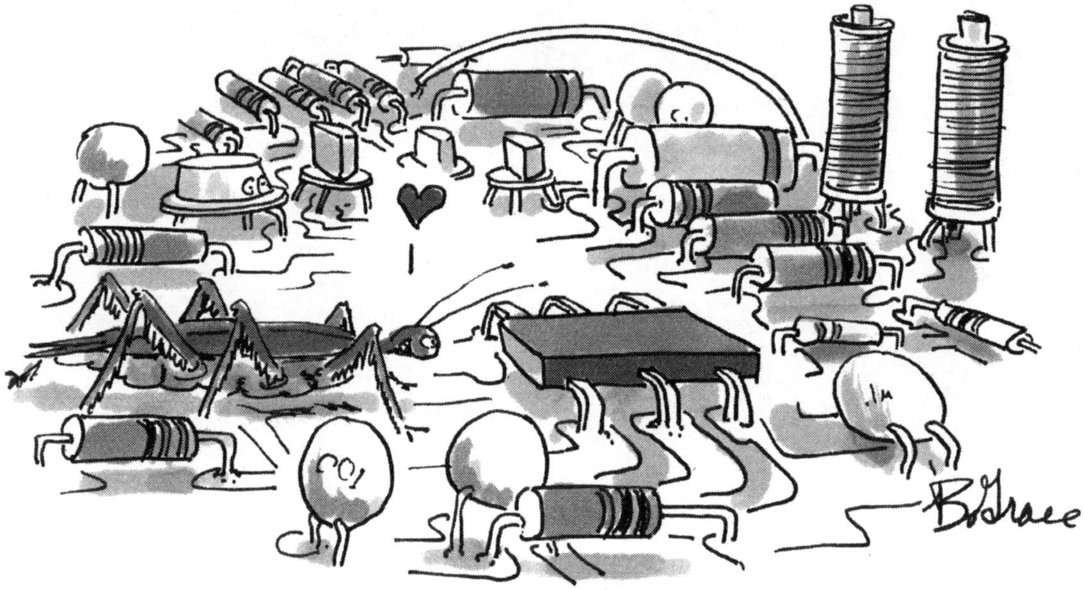

"Gee, and all this time I thought Physical Review was a girlie magazine."

"Bear in mind, Professor Boswick, there is a fine line between genius and insanity."

Physics Professors telling dirty stories
β(ω)=−[a(z)/3][2χDM(Δ,z)
+2χDM^zz(0,z)−2χDPD(0,z)
+ BIG BOOBS +2χDPD(Δ,z)
−χDD^H(Δ,z)]
B. Grace

"Now all we need is isotonic vermuth

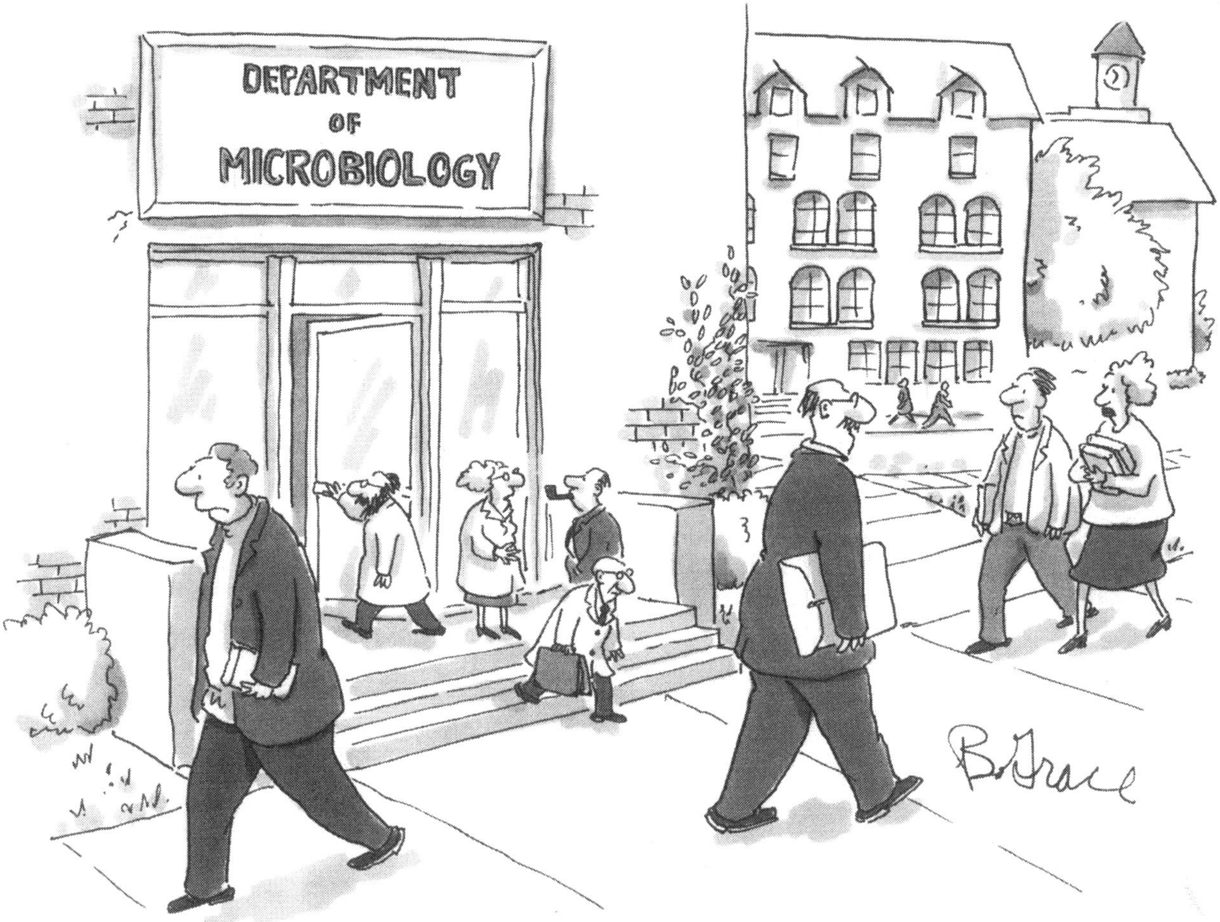
DEPARTMENT
OF
MICROBIOLOGY
B. Grace

"The antiagression drug looks promising, but we'll need more research money. Steinmetz just freed the rats."

"What this laboratory really needs is better ventilation."

"Now if we can just get you on Oprah and improve your credibility."

"I hate these behavior modification lab mixers."

"I will, of course, be grading on a curve."

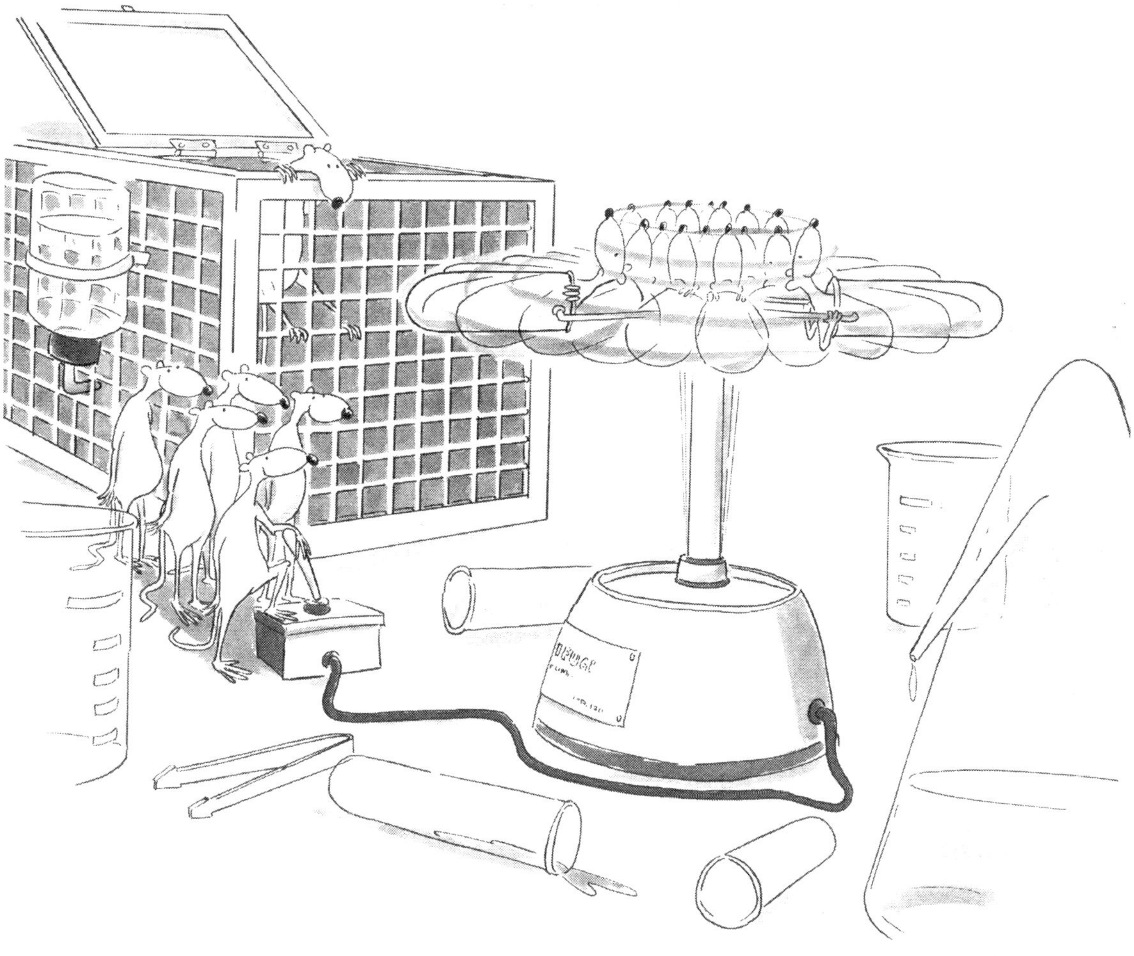

"On the bright side, we now know the rest mass of an antinose particle."

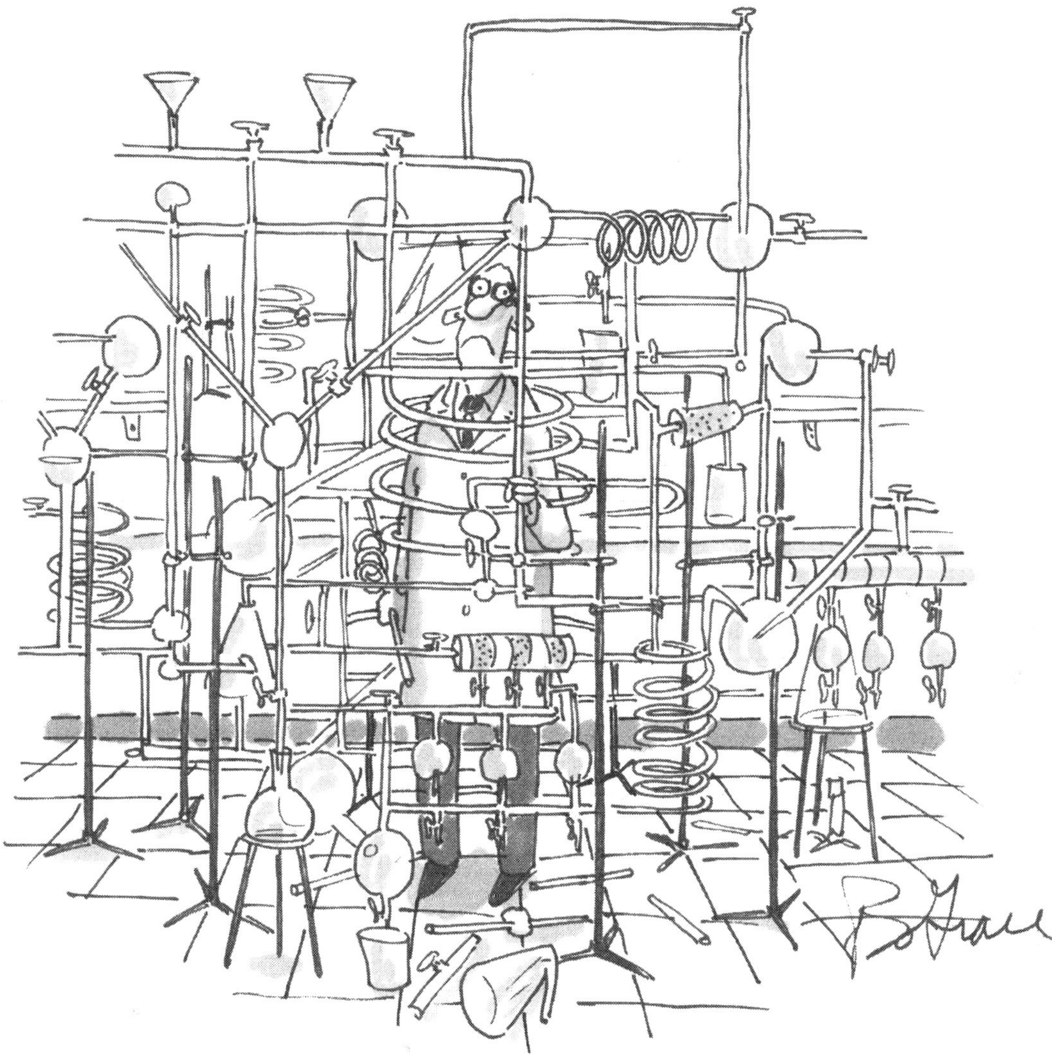

"Enough theatrics, Steinmetz! Show us some numbers!"

"Between you and me, Professor Stienwert, I'd assign Biglow a charge zero, spin zero, charm zero, and strangeness about a nine point five."

"What this laboratory really needs is better ventilation."

"So that's your secret."

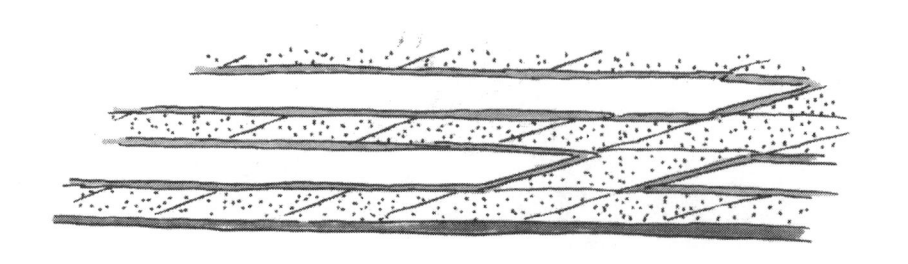

"Remarkable determination. He's spent his entire career trying to discover antigravity."

"... And what we first believed to be the 'Shroud of Bayonne' turned out to be a bowling towel owned by Mr. Herman Nodolski of Patterson, New Jersey"

DOES ANYBODY KNOW HOW TO WORK THIS COFFEE MACHINE?
THOSE THINGS ARE BEYOND ME
DON'T LOOK AT ME
I CAN'T WORK THOSE CONTRAPTIONS
NO CAN DO
NOT ME
ME EITHER

"Well he **ought** to be surprised. That thing's a coelacanth."

"Not only did I steal the chips, I also picked up some clam dip."

"Professor Nusbaum's 'been around' alright. He just spent two years in Belize studying terrestrial monopods."

"I'm not surprised. Professor Wozinski is well known for his unconventional gambits."

"We think his brain is stuck in a do-loop."

"Thank God it's a vegetarian."

"Frankly, I think he's trying to cover up a shaky theory."

"Well, dynamite fired power plants aren't the answer."

"You push the first switch down,
 And the protons go round and round,
 Oh-oh-oh-ohhh-oh-oh,
 And they come out here."

"Eh! Galileo! What'sa theese biga blacka ring arounda my eye?!"

fin

Made in the USA
Middletown, DE
24 September 2018